SHIFT HAPPENS

Small Mindset Changes. Big Life Results.

by
LaTarsha Mills-McKie

© 2025 LaTarsha Mills-McKie
All rights reserved.

© 2025 LaTarsha Mills-McKie
All rights reserved.

No part of this book may be reproduced, stored in a retrieval system, or transmitted in any form or by any means — electronic, mechanical, photocopying, recording, or otherwise — without prior written permission from the author.

For educational and personal development use only.

Published in the United States of America
First Edition, 2025

ISBN: **979-8-218-86568-9**

Cover Design: Designed by the Author
Interior Layout: LaTarsha Mills-McKie

www.CoachLatarsha.com

Dedication

For every person who's ever felt stuck, uncertain, or afraid to begin again — this is your reminder that small shifts create powerful change.

Acknowledgments

This book was born from the stories, courage, and resilience of every person I've had the privilege to coach and teach.

To my parents, family, friends, and mentors — thank you for believing in my vision, even before I did.

To Amir and Jalal, my heart and my soul, you have inspired me in ways you'll never know!

To every reader: thank you for saying "yes" to your growth.

Keep showing up. Keep shifting.

Table of Contents

Introduction: What SHIFT really means………......………… i
Chapter 1 See the Lens: Fixed vs. Growth………..........…… 1
Chapter 2 Get Clear on What You Want………….....…..…… 9
Chapter 3 Choose Your Daily Focus: Attention is Your Advantage………………………………………….…………… 14
Chapter 4 Small Wins Trigger Momentum and Motivation..20
Chapter 5 Shifting Through the Bounce Back: Fail Smarter, Not Harder………………………………………………....…..25
Chapter 6 Stay in the Shift: Make it stick……… ……..……. 31
Conclusion Your Shift, Your Life………....…….…………..…36
Resource Library……………................………………….…… 42
About the author ……………………………………......…......…46

"Shift Happens — not by accident, but by intention."

— LaTarsha Mills-McKie | Shift Happens

Shift Happens: Small Mindset Shifts, Big Life Results

Book Promise

By the end, readers will understand what mindset is, how it forms and how to shift it—one thought at a time—using simple, evidence-based practices that create real life results.

Introduction: What "Shift" Really Means

When most people hear the word *shift*, they think of something dramatic—a major life overhaul, a sudden transformation, or a leap from where they are to where they want to be. But in reality, a shift is something much more approachable, and often much more powerful.

A shift is a **small, intentional change in perspective, thought, or behavior** that nudges your life in a new direction. It's not about forcing yourself into being someone else—it's about adjusting the lens you're already looking through so you can see opportunities, possibilities, and solutions that were always there, waiting to be noticed.

Think of a shift like adjusting the steering wheel while driving. You don't need to yank it dramatically to stay on course; small, consistent corrections keep you moving toward your destination. The same is true for your mindset.

This book is about those shifts—the simple but transformative changes that help you move from where you are to where you want to be. With each chapter, you'll uncover practical tools, grounded in research and real-life application, that show you how shifting your thoughts by just a few degrees can create powerful ripple effects across your relationships, career, health, and personal fulfillment.

Shift happens when you choose it. You don't need a perfect plan, the right timing, or someone else's approval. You just need the willingness to see things differently, one thought at a time.

By the end of this journey, you'll understand that change isn't as far away as it seems. It's already within you—waiting for a shift.

What Is Mindset?

Your **mindset** is the collection of thoughts, beliefs, and attitudes that shape how you see yourself, others, and the world around you. It's like the operating system of your mind—it runs in the background, influencing how you interpret experiences, respond to challenges, and make decisions.

A mindset isn't just what you think; it's **how you think**. It filters every situation you face: whether you see failure as a setback or a lesson, whether you approach change with fear or curiosity, whether you believe your abilities are fixed or capable of growth.

In short:

- **Mindset is the lens you look through.**
- **Mindset determines what you notice and what you overlook.**
- **Mindset drives your choices—and your results.**

The powerful truth is that your mindset is not fixed. You can shift it, strengthen it, and shape it to serve the life you want to create.

Why Small Changes Work: Compounding Effects and Neuroplasticity

When people think about transforming their lives, they often imagine making massive, sweeping changes—quitting a job overnight, overhauling their health routines, or reinventing themselves completely. But the truth is, **lasting change rarely comes from giant leaps. It comes from small, steady shifts repeated over time.**

1. The Compounding Effect
Think of small changes like financial investments. A single deposit may not seem like much, but over time, consistent contributions grow into something significant because of compounding interest. Your mindset works the same way. Choosing a more empowering thought today, practicing gratitude tomorrow, or responding with curiosity instead of frustration may seem minor in the moment—but repeated daily, these micro-shifts accumulate into major transformations in how you think, feel, and act.

2. Neuroplasticity: Your Brain's Ability to Rewire
Neuroscience confirms this truth through a concept called **neuroplasticity**—the brain's ability to form and strengthen new neural pathways. Every time you think a thought or practice a behavior, your brain fires a pattern of neurons. Repetition reinforces the pathway, making it stronger and easier to access next time.

This means:

- Old, unhelpful patterns can weaken when you stop using them.
- New, healthier patterns can grow stronger with practice.
- Small, consistent changes literally rewire your brain to work in your favor.

Neuroplasticity: Your Brain Can Change

The concept of **neuroplasticity**—is the brain's ability to reorganize itself by forming new neural connections throughout life. In simple terms: **your brain changes with practice.**

A famous study by **Draganski et al. (2004)** showed just how powerful this can be. Researchers taught a group of adults how to juggle—something none of them had done before. After three months of practice, brain scans revealed that the regions responsible for **visual and motor coordination** had actually grown in size. When the participants stopped practicing, those areas shrank back.

This study proved something revolutionary:

- Learning a new skill doesn't just change what you *know*—it physically changes your brain.
- Repetition strengthens neural pathways, making behaviors and thought patterns easier over time.
- Stopping practice weakens those connections, which is why consistency matters.

What this means for you is powerful: every small mindset shift you practice—choosing gratitude, reframing failure, pausing before reacting—literally reshapes your brain. Over time, those small shifts become your new defaults.

Your brain is built to change. And that means you are never stuck.

3. The Shift Multiplies
The beauty of small changes is that they don't stay small. Over time, they create ripple effects: more confidence, better decisions, healthier habits, stronger relationships. One small mindset shift can trigger a cascade of positive outcomes that may seem almost effortless—because your brain, once rewired, begins to work *with* you instead of against you.

In short: Small changes work because they build momentum, reshape your brain, and multiply over time. That's the power of a shift.

How to Use This Book

This book isn't meant to be something you simply read and put back on the shelf. It's designed to be a **practical guide**—a tool you can use to create real change in your daily life.

Here's how to get the most out of it:

1. Read with Curiosity
Each chapter introduces a mindset principle and shows you what it means to "shift" in that area. Don't rush through it—take your time to reflect on what resonates and notice where you may already see opportunities for growth.

2. Apply One Micro-Shift at a Time
At the end of every chapter, you'll find a simple, doable action step—a micro-shift. These aren't overwhelming or complicated; they're small adjustments you can practice right away. Choose **one shift per week** to focus on.

3. Track Your Results
Keep a notebook, journal, or even a notes app handy to record your experiences. Ask yourself:

- What did I notice this week when I applied this shift?
- How did it affect my mood, choices, or relationships?
- What feels easier now than before?

Over time, you'll build your own record of transformation—a map of how small mindset shifts have created big results.

4. Give Yourself Permission to Repeat
Some shifts may click instantly, while others may take longer to feel natural. That's okay. This isn't about perfection—it's about practice. Return to a shift as often

as you need until it becomes part of your natural way of thinking.

5. Trust the Process
You may not notice massive change overnight—but remember, big results come from small, consistent steps. Week by week, thought by thought, you're rewiring your brain and reshaping your life.

Chapter 1 – See the Lens: Fixed vs. Growth in Real Life

Before you can shift your mindset, you first need to **see the lens you're looking through**. Every one of us filters life through a set of beliefs that shape how we interpret challenges, effort, feedback, and setbacks. Psychologist Carol Dweck calls these lenses the **fixed mindset** and the **growth mindset**.

Growth Mindset (Dweck, 2006)

In her groundbreaking research, psychologist **Dr. Carol Dweck (2006)** introduced the concepts of *fixed mindset* and *growth mindset*. These two ways of thinking powerfully shape how we approach challenges, learning, and personal development.

- **Fixed Mindset**: The belief that intelligence, talent, and ability are *set traits*—you either have them, or you don't. In this mindset, failure feels like a reflection of your worth, so people tend to avoid risks, challenges, or feedback.
- **Growth Mindset**: The belief that intelligence and abilities can be **developed through effort, learning, and persistence**. In this mindset, failure isn't proof you can't do something—it's

- evidence that you're learning and an opportunity to grow.

Why does this matter? Because your mindset influences:

- **How you see obstacles** – as roadblocks or as steppingstones.
- **How you handle failure** – as the end of the story or as a lesson.
- **How you view effort** – as a waste of time or as the path to mastery.

Research shows that people who adopt a growth mindset are **more resilient, more motivated, and more successful** in school, work, sports, and relationships. The good news? A growth mindset isn't something you're born with—it's something you can *choose* and strengthen with practice.

The Power of Seeing the Lens

When you start noticing your own inner dialogue, you'll see which lens you're looking through. The good news is that you're not locked into one or the other—you can learn to shift from a fixed to a growth mindset one thought at a time.

The lens you use matters—because it changes how you think, how you feel, and ultimately, what actions you take.

Let's break down how each mindset interprets common experiences:

Chapter Objective: Name Your Default Lens and Spot It in the World

By the end of this chapter, you should be able to:

1. **Identify your default lens** — notice whether you lean more often toward a fixed mindset or a growth mindset.
2. **Spot your lens in action** — catch the language, reactions, and habits that reveal how your mindset is shaping your choices.

Exercise: My Default Lens

Step 1 – Reflection
Think of a situation from the past week where you faced:

- A challenge
- Feedback
- A mistake or setback

Write a quick note about how you responded:

- Situation:
  _____
- My reaction:
  _____
- Lens I used: ☐ Fixed ☐ Growth

Step 2 – Patterns

- When do I most often notice a fixed mindset showing up?

  _____

- When do I naturally lean toward a growth mindset?

  _____

Step 3 – Spot It in the World
Pay attention this week to conversations, media, or workplace/interactions. Where do you hear fixed or growth language?

- Fixed mindset example I noticed:
  _____
- Growth mindset example I noticed:
  _____

☑ Language Audit: The Words That Shape Your Mindset

Your words are powerful. They don't just describe your reality—they help create it. The language you use with yourself (self-talk) and others can reveal whether you're operating from a **fixed** or **growth** mindset.

This simple audit helps you spot "fixed" language and shift it into "growth" language.

Step 1: Notice Fixed Mindset Phrases

Here are common examples of fixed mindset language:

- "I'm just not good at this."
- "That's just the way I am."
- "If I have to try, it means I'm not talented."
- "I can't handle failure."
- "I'll never be able to…"

Step 2: Reframe Into Growth Language

Here's how those same statements can shift:

- **Fixed:** "I'm just not good at this."
  Growth: "I'm still learning. I can get better with practice."

- **Fixed:** "That's just the way I am."
  Growth: "I'm capable of change and growth."
- **Fixed:** "If I have to try, it means I'm not talented."
  Growth: "Effort is how I develop my talents."
- **Fixed:** "I can't handle failure."
  Growth: "Failure is feedback. It shows me what to adjust."
- **Fixed:** "I'll never be able to…"
  Growth: "I haven't mastered this *yet*."

Key Takeaway: Awareness is the first shift. Once you can name your lens and spot it in action—both in yourself and in the world—you gain the power to choose differently.

🏀 Real-Life Example: Michael Jordan — Turning Rejection into Motivation

The Situation:
As a sophomore, Michael Jordan was *cut from his high school varsity basketball team.*
He was devastated. His first reaction was disappointment and embarrassment — it felt like failure. But what came next defined his legacy.

The Shift:
Instead of seeing being cut as a *final verdict* on his talent, Jordan reframed it as *feedback*. He asked himself:

"What do I really want — and how much am I willing to work for it?"

That clarity gave him purpose. He realized he didn't just want to "make the team"; he wanted to *become great.*

So, he made a decision:

- He trained relentlessly every morning and evening.
- He used the memory of that cut list as *fuel* instead of *proof* of defeat.
- He focused on growth — developing his skills, mindset, and resilience.

The Result:
By his senior year, Jordan not only made the varsity team but became a standout player. His mindset shift from *rejection → determination* carried him all the way through college, the NBA, and into global icon status.

💡 Mindset Shift Lesson:

Fixed Mindset: "I wasn't good enough, so I failed."
Growth Mindset: "I wasn't ready *yet,* but I can get better."

Jordan didn't let one "no" define him. He used it to get clear on what he wanted (to be the best) — and *why it mattered* (to prove to himself that his potential was limitless).

Chapter 2 – Get Clear on What You Want (and Why It Matters)

In Chapter 1, you learned how to spot the lens you're looking through. Now it's time to **point that lens in the right direction.** The truth is, you can't shift what you don't define. Clarity about what you want—and why it matters—is the starting line for every transformation.

Without clarity, your energy scatters. You react to life instead of creating it. But when you know what you want, your brain gets a target. Neuroscience shows that the brain is wired to pursue goals: when you set a clear intention, your **reticular activating system (RAS)**—the brain's built-in filter—starts scanning for people, resources, and opportunities that match your focus.

What Do You Really Want?

This is about *your* wants—not what other people expect from you. Ask yourself:

- Where in my life do I feel most restless or unfulfilled?
- If nothing could stop me, what would I go after?
- What would "better" look like for me right now?

Why Does It Matter?

Your *why* anchors you. A weak "why" fades when life gets hard. A strong "why" keeps you moving, even when obstacles, self-doubt, or failure show up.

Try this: Write down what you want. Then ask yourself three times: **"Why does this matter to me?"** Each time, go deeper. By the third answer, you'll uncover the true fuel behind your goal.

How a Growth Mindset Helps You Get BIG Life Results

This is where mindset comes in. Having a goal is powerful—but whether you *reach it* depends on the lens you use to pursue it.

- **Fixed Mindset Approach:** "If I don't succeed quickly, I must not be good enough." Results are limited because effort feels like proof of weakness.
- **Growth Mindset Approach:** "Every step—win or setback—is part of the process. The more I learn, the closer I get." Results expand because effort fuels growth.

A growth mindset helps you get BIG life results because it shifts how you handle the entire journey:

- **Challenges?** Opportunities to stretch.
- **Effort?** The path to mastery.
- **Feedback?** Free coaching.
- **Setbacks?** Temporary data, not permanent failure.

When you combine **clarity** (knowing what you want and why) with a **growth mindset** (believing you can develop the skills and habits to get there), you create unstoppable momentum. This is the formula for BIG life results—results that ripple into your confidence, relationships, career, and overall sense of purpose.

Reflection Exercise: The Clarity Map

1. **Area of focus (relationships, career, financial freedom, etc.):**
   _____

2. **What I want (in one clear sentence):**
   _____

3. **Why it matters (three layers deep):**
   1. _____
   2. _____
   3. _____

4. **Mindset check:** Which lens am I bringing to this goal?
   ☐ Fixed ☐ Growth ☐ A mix of both

✅ **Key Takeaway:** Clarity gives you direction. Growth mindset gives you fuel. Together, they create the shifts that lead to the results you want and deserve.

Real Life Example: Meet Jasmine:
Jasmine was a high school counselor who often said, "I just want a better job." She felt exhausted and undervalued but wasn't sure what "better" meant. Her vague goal left her spinning her wheels — she browsed job boards, applied to random openings, and even considered leaving education altogether.

One day, she paused and asked herself the two key questions from this chapter:

1. **What do I really want?**
2. **Why does it matter to me?**

At first, she listed surface goals: higher pay, more flexibility, less stress. But as she dug deeper, she realized her *why* was about impact — she wanted to help *more students thrive without burning herself out*.

That clarity shifted everything. She stopped chasing job titles and started looking for roles that aligned with her values: student growth, innovation, and balance. Within months, she applied for and landed a **District SEL Coordinator** position. It offered the same salary but greater purpose and creative freedom — exactly what she was craving.

Her shift:
☞ *From focusing on what she wanted to escape (stress, exhaustion)*
☞ *To focusing on what she wanted to create (impact, alignment, and joy)*

💡 Lesson:

When your *why* is clear, your *what* becomes more intentional — and your actions gain direction.
Clarity turns scattered effort into focused momentum.

Chapter 3 – Choose Your Daily Focus: Attention is Your Advantage

Where your attention goes, your energy flows.

Clarity gives you the big picture of what you want and why it matters. But big results are built **one day at a time**. That's why learning to direct your daily focus is one of the most powerful shifts you can make.

Attention Is Your Advantage

Your attention is like a spotlight. Whatever you shine it on grows brighter in your life. If you focus on problems, setbacks, and limitations—you'll see more of them. If you focus on progress, opportunities, and possibilities—you'll start noticing them everywhere.

Psychologists call this the **attentional filter**. Once you decide something matters, your brain highlights it—like how you suddenly notice the same car everywhere right after you buy one. This means **you get to choose what your brain spotlights.**

Science Spotlight: Implementation Intentions

It's one thing to know what you want. It's another thing to follow through. Research shows that one of the most effective ways to bridge the gap between intention and action is to use **implementation intentions**—a strategy studied by psychologist Peter Gollwitzer and colleagues.

An **implementation intention** is a simple *if–then* plan that links a specific situation to a specific behavior. For example:

- "If it's 7:00 a.m., then I will put on my walking shoes and go outside."
- "If I get nervous before speaking up in a meeting, then I will take one deep breath and remind myself I've prepared."
- "If I feel tempted to quit, then I will read my why statement."

Why does this work? Because you're not just setting a vague goal ("I want to exercise more"). You're pre-programming your brain with a clear response for a predictable situation. That way, when the trigger moment arrives, you don't waste energy deciding what to do—you simply act.

The Results: Studies consistently show that people who use implementation intentions are **far more likely to achieve their goals** than those who rely on willpower alone. In fact, meta-analyses reveal significant improvements in everything from exercise habits to academic performance to healthy eating when people adopt this strategy.

Daily Focus as a Shift Practice

Big life results don't come from doing everything at once. They come from choosing one shift at a time and practicing it with intention.

Each day, ask yourself:

- *What is the one thought, belief, or action I want to focus on today?*
- *If I only did this one thing, would it move me closer to who I want to become?*

This keeps your energy directed instead of scattered.

Micro-Shifts in Action

- Instead of focusing on "not enough time," shift to "I can use the time I do have wisely."
- Instead of focusing on "I always mess up," shift to "I'm learning and improving every time."
- Instead of focusing on "I can't handle this," shift to "I can take the next step."

Reflection Exercise: My Daily Focus

1. Today, my focus is:
   _____
2. This matters because:
   _____

3. At the end of the day, I'll know I honored this focus if: _____

✅ **Key Takeaway:** You don't need to control everything—you just need to control your focus. Each day you choose where to place your attention, you are actively rewiring your brain, building new habits, and embracing the goal and shift.

Implementation intentions make your goals actionable. Instead of relying on motivation in the moment, you set up clear mental instructions in advance—giving yourself the best chance to follow through and see results.

🎯 **Real-Life Example: Serena Williams — Winning One Point at a Time**

The Situation:
Serena Williams, one of the greatest tennis players in history, has faced incredible pressure on the world stage — championship points, setbacks, even public criticism. Yet, when asked how she handles it all, she often says:

"I just focus on the next point."

Serena learned that letting her mind drift to the scoreboard, the crowd, or her mistakes only distracted her. When she narrowed her attention to *the one point right in front of her*, her performance sharpened — her focus became her advantage.

The Shift:
Instead of spreading her energy across everything she *couldn't control* (the opponent, the outcome, or the media), she trained her attention on what she *could control* — her breathing, her stance, her next swing.

That intentional focus became her edge. It's how she rebounded from losses, staged legendary comebacks, and maintained mental clarity through decades of competition.

The Lesson:
Your attention is your most valuable resource.
Where your attention goes, your energy flows.

When you choose your daily focus — whether it's *staying calm during chaos*, *finishing one meaningful task*, or *showing up as your best self* — you shift from being reactive to being intentional.

Mindset Shift:

Scattered Attention: "I have so much to do — I don't know where to start."
Focused Attention: "I'll win *this* moment. One point at a time."

Reflection Prompt (for your workbook page):

- What's one focus that would make today a win for you?
- What distractions tend to pull your attention away?
- How can you gently bring your focus back when your mind wanders?

Chapter 4 – Small Wins Trigger Momentum and Motivation

When we think about motivation, we often imagine huge breakthroughs—landing the promotion, hitting the weight loss goal, running the marathon. But research shows that the real driver of motivation is much smaller and much closer to home: **progress.**

In their landmark study, *The Progress Principle* (Amabile & Kramer, 2010), researchers found that the single most powerful factor boosting motivation, engagement, and even happiness at work wasn't money, recognition, or big achievements—it was making consistent progress on meaningful work. In other words, **small wins spark big momentum.**

Why Small Wins Matter

- **Momentum Builder:** Each small success signals to your brain, *"I'm moving forward."* That creates energy to keep going.
- **Confidence Booster:** Small wins build self-belief. Each one whispers, *"See? You can do this."*
- **Motivation Multiplier:** Progress fuels intrinsic motivation—the desire to keep going because the work itself feels rewarding.

Intrinsic Motivation: The Lasting Fuel

Extrinsic rewards (praise, money, external approval) can help in the short term, but intrinsic motivation is what keeps you going long after the external rewards fade. When you feel proud of your progress and energized by the process itself, you don't have to force motivation—it flows naturally.

The Power of Micro-Shifts

This is where your daily mindset practice pays off. Each time you:

- Reframe a negative thought
- Respond with patience instead of frustration
- Stick with a new habit for one more day

…you create a small win. Over time, those small wins build momentum. And momentum creates transformation.

Reflection Exercise: Track Your Wins

This week, keep a running list of your **small wins.** No matter how tiny they seem, write them down.

- Today I made progress by:
  _____
- One thing I'm proud of:
  _____

- Because of this win, I feel:
  _____

At the end of the week, look back at your list. Notice how many wins you've collected—proof that progress is happening, one shift at a time.

Key Takeaway: Small wins matter more than you think. They don't just mark progress—they create the momentum and motivation you need to keep moving toward BIG life results.

Real-Life Example: James Clear — Building Atomic Habits One Percent at a Time

The Situation:
Before becoming a bestselling author, James Clear wasn't a productivity expert or motivational speaker. He was a college baseball player recovering from a devastating injury that left him uncertain about his future.

During recovery, James realized he couldn't control everything — but he *could* control his **daily habits**. Instead of setting huge, overwhelming goals, he focused on *small wins* each day: showing up to rehab, doing one more rep, reading for 10 minutes, writing a single paragraph.

The Shift:
Those small wins didn't look impressive day-to-day. But

over time, they built powerful momentum — his body healed, his confidence grew, and his focus sharpened.

Years later, that same philosophy became the foundation of his book *Atomic Habits*, based on the principle that:

"Tiny changes produce remarkable results."

The Result:
His "1% better every day" approach has helped millions of people improve their health, careers, and relationships. The key wasn't perfection — it was progress.

Mindset Shift:

Old Thinking: "Big results require big effort."
Shifted Mindset: "Small consistent wins compound into big success."

The Lesson:

Each small win — finishing a workout, sending the email you've been avoiding, meditating for five minutes — tells your brain, *"I'm capable."* That sense of progress sparks motivation, which fuels more action.

Momentum is built, not found.

Chapter 5 – Shifting Through the Bounce Back: Fail Smarter, Not Harder

Failure is not the opposite of success—it's the pathway to it. Embracing the "shift" will have setbacks and failures, but what will you do not if, but when this happens? Every person who has achieved big life results has also experienced setbacks, mistakes, and detours. The difference isn't whether you fail, it's how you bounce back.

Reframing Failure with a Growth Mindset

A **fixed mindset** interprets failure as proof of inadequacy: *"I'm not good enough. I'll never succeed."* A **growth mindset** interprets failure as feedback: *"That didn't work—yet. What can I learn and try differently next time?"*

When you embrace failure as information instead of identity, you shift from shame to strategy.

The words you use to describe failure shape how you experience it. A fixed mindset sees failure as *final*; a growth mindset sees failure as *feedback*.

Here's how to reframe:

Fixed Mindset Response	Growth Mindset Reframe
"I'm terrible at this."	"I'm still learning this."
"This didn't work, so I failed."	"This didn't work, so I discovered one way that doesn't fit yet."
"I'll never be good at this."	"I'm not good at this *yet*—but I can improve with practice."
"That mistake proves I don't belong."	"That mistake is teaching me what I need to grow."
"I wasted my time."	"I invested time in learning what doesn't work—next time will be smarter."

The Bounce Back Cycle

Resilient people follow a simple loop when they face setbacks:

1. **Pause** – Acknowledge the disappointment. (No toxic positivity—feel it honestly.)
2. **Process** – Extract the lesson. What worked? What didn't?
3. **Pivot** – Apply the lesson to your next attempt.

The faster you move through this loop, the smarter—not harder—your bounce back becomes.

Reflection Exercise: Fail Smarter Journal

Think of a recent setback and walk it through the Bounce Back Cycle:

- **Pause** – How did I feel?
  _____
- **Process** – What did this experience teach me?
  _____
- **Pivot** – What will I do differently next time?
  _____

✅ **Key Takeaway:** When you change the story you tell yourself about failure, you unlock resilience. Reframing isn't pretending—it's choosing to see failure as part of progress instead of proof you can't succeed.

Failure is not a dead end—it's data. When you fail smarter, each setback becomes a steppingstone toward the results you want.

💬 **Real-Life Example: Oprah Winfrey — Reframing Rejection into Redirection**

The Situation:
Before becoming a global media icon, Oprah Winfrey was *fired* from her first television job as a news anchor in Baltimore.
Her producer told her she was "unfit for television."

26

For a young, ambitious woman who had dreamed of broadcasting since childhood, that moment felt like failure. She was devastated — embarrassed, unsure, and tempted to quit the industry entirely.

The Shift:
Instead of letting rejection define her, Oprah asked herself:

"What can I learn from this — and how can I grow through it?"

She realized that reading scripted news wasn't her strength — but connecting deeply with people *was*. That insight helped her pivot from traditional news to human-interest storytelling. She leaned into authenticity and empathy — the very traits that got her fired — and turned them into her superpowers.

The Result:
That so-called "failure" became the turning point that led to *The Oprah Winfrey Show*, one of the most successful talk shows in television history.

Her bounce back wasn't about working harder to fit someone else's mold — it was about working *smarter* by aligning with her strengths, values, and purpose.

Mindset Shift

Old Thinking	Shifted Mindset
"I failed — I'm not good enough."	"This didn't work — what can I learn and adjust?"

The Lesson

Failure isn't the opposite of success — it's *part* of success.
When you fail smarter, you:

- Treat mistakes as information, not identity.
- Look for lessons instead of losses.
- Adjust your strategy without abandoning your vision.

Every setback becomes a setup for a comeback — *if you're willing to learn from it.*

Reflection: Your Turn

- What's a time you thought you failed but later realized it taught you something valuable?
- What feedback or insight did that experience give you?
- How can you apply those lessons to "bounce back better" today?

Chapter 6 – Stay in the Shift: Make It Stick

Making a shift is powerful. But keeping the shift—that's where transformation happens.

It's easy to get inspired by a new idea, habit, or mindset. The challenge is sticking with it long enough for it to become second nature. Neuroscience tells us that every repeated thought and action literally strengthens the wiring in your brain. The more you practice a shift, the more automatic it becomes.

Why Sticking Matters

- **Habits outlast motivation.** Motivation fluctuates, but habits keep you grounded.
- **Consistency rewires your brain.** Each repetition strengthens the neural pathway of your new mindset.
- **Momentum compounds.** One day of practice is progress. Thirty days of practice is transformation and habit forming.

Strategies to Stay in the Shift

1. **Anchor to Your Why**
   Remind yourself often *why* this shift matters to you. A strong "why" sustains you when willpower dips.

2. **Stack It on a Habit**
   Use habit stacking: tie your new shift to something you already do.
   - o "After I pour my morning coffee, I'll write my daily focus."
   - o "When I close my laptop at work, I'll write one small win."
3. **Track It to Reinforce It**
   Recording progress—even in small ways—signals success to your brain and builds momentum.
4. **Celebrate the Micro-Milestones**
   Each week you stay in the shift is worth celebrating. Intrinsic motivation grows when you acknowledge progress.

Reflection Exercise: My Stick Strategy

- My chosen shift:
  _____
- Why it matters:
  _____
- The habit I'll stack it with:
  _____
- How I'll track progress:
  _____
- How I'll celebrate:
  _____

☑ **Key Takeaway:** Lasting change doesn't come from one big leap—it comes from small, steady shifts practiced over time. Stay in the shift long enough, and the shift becomes who you are.

🔄 **Real-Life Example: Dwayne "The Rock" Johnson — Turning Discipline Into a Lifestyle**

The Situation:
Before becoming one of the most successful actors and entrepreneurs in the world, Dwayne "The Rock" Johnson faced a massive setback.
At 23, his dream of playing professional football ended when he was cut from the Canadian Football League. He had $7 in his pocket, no job, and no clear path forward.

For a while, he battled disappointment and self-doubt — but then, he decided to **stay in the shift.**

The Shift:
Instead of letting that failure define him, The Rock chose to redefine himself.
He realized that if he wanted a different life, he had to *live differently every day.*

He turned to fitness and discipline as anchors — waking up early, training hard, and writing out his goals daily. Over time, those habits didn't just rebuild his body; they rebuilt his mindset.

His consistency became his confidence.
He often says:

"Success isn't about greatness. It's about consistency. Consistent hard work gains success. Greatness will come."

The Result:
That daily commitment — staying in the shift — transformed him from a failed athlete into a global brand, actor, and motivational figure. His success wasn't a one-time burst of motivation; it was built on daily choices that aligned with his bigger vision.

 **Mindset Shift**

Old Thinking	Shifted Mindset
"I'll change when I feel motivated."	"I'll stay consistent — and motivation will follow."

⚡ The Lesson

Change doesn't stick because you *want* it — it sticks because you *work it.*
Staying in the shift means:

- Building habits that reinforce who you want to become.
- Revisiting your "why" when things get hard.
- Progressing even on the days you don't feel like it.

Real transformation happens when your *new mindset becomes your normal.*

📝 Reflection: Your Turn

- What's one habit that helps you stay in your shift?
- How can you remind yourself of your "why" when motivation fades?
- What does "showing up anyway" look like for you this week?

Conclusion – Your Shift, Your Life

Congratulations. By reading this book and engaging with the exercises, you've already begun the most important step: **awareness.** You've learned how to:

- See the lens you're looking through—fixed or growth.
- Get clear on what you want and why it matters.
- Choose your daily focus and direct your attention intentionally.
- Use implementation intentions to turn goals into action.
- Celebrate small wins and build momentum.
- Fail smarter and bounce back stronger.
- Stay in the shift long enough to make it stick.

Each chapter has given you **micro-shifts**—small, actionable steps that may feel minor in the moment, but over time, compound into **BIG life results**.

Change doesn't begin in the world around you — it begins in the world *within* you.

Every breakthrough, every success, every moment of growth starts with a single thought that dares to see things differently.
That's what *Shift Happens* is all about — learning how

to pause, pivot, and practice a mindset that moves you closer to the life you want.

You've discovered that mindset isn't magic — it's muscle.
And like any muscle, it strengthens with use.

When you *get clear* on what you want and why it matters, you align your focus.
When you *choose your daily attention,* you gain control over your energy.
When you *celebrate small wins,* you build momentum and confidence.
When you *fail smarter,* you turn setbacks into feedback.
When you *stay in the shift,* you transform consistency into identity.

Bit by bit, shift by shift, you've learned how to move from reaction to intention, from limitation to possibility. You've proven that small changes in thinking create powerful changes in living.

The Truth About the Shift

Shifting your mindset isn't about becoming someone new — it's about *returning to who you truly are* when fear, doubt, and limitation fall away.
It's the practice of choosing alignment over anxiety, progress over perfection, and growth over guilt.

You won't always get it right.
There will be days you slip back into old patterns — that's okay.
The shift is a practice, not a performance. What matters is that you *notice it sooner* and *return to your truth faster*.

⚡ Final Thought:

Your life shifts the moment *you do*.

So keep choosing thoughts that empower you.
Keep practicing awareness over autopilot.
Keep celebrating progress, no matter how small.

You have everything you need to design the life you want — one mindset, one moment, one shift at a time.

🎤 Real-Life Example: Mel Robbins — From Stuck to Self-Driven

The Situation:
Years before becoming a bestselling author and motivational speaker, Mel Robbins was at one of the lowest points in her life.
She was unemployed, drowning in debt, and struggling with anxiety. Every morning she'd hit snooze — not just on her alarm, but on her life.

She knew she *needed* to change, but she didn't *feel* motivated to. The more she waited for inspiration, the more stuck she felt.

The Shift:
One night, she saw a rocket launch on TV and thought:

"That's what I need — to launch myself out of bed like a rocket."

The next morning, she counted down: "5-4-3-2-1" — and stood up before her mind could talk her out of it.

That small action — a mental interruption — was the start of her shift. She began using the **5 Second Rule** to take immediate action instead of overthinking or procrastinating.

The Result:
That simple shift rewired how she made decisions, built confidence, and took ownership of her life.
It led her to rebuild her career, write multiple bestsellers, and inspire millions to take small actions toward big change.

Mel's transformation wasn't luck — it was *leadership over her own mind*.

 **Mindset Shift**

Old Thinking	Shifted Mindset
"I'll change when I feel ready."	"I create readiness through action."

⚡ The Lesson

Your life changes when you stop waiting for the right moment — and start creating it.

Each time you choose a new thought, take a brave step, or respond differently than before, you rewrite your story.
Your shift isn't just about changing your mind; it's about *changing your life — one decision at a time.*

🔺 Reflection: Your Turn

- What's one mindset shift that has already changed how you show up?
- How has that shift impacted your relationships, confidence, or peace of mind?
- What's one daily choice you can make to live out your new mindset?

Because when your mindset shifts…
⚡ **your life follows.**

📚 Shift Happens Resource Library

Practical tools, science-based insights, and mindset exercises from the book — all in one place.

"Growth doesn't happen by accident. It happens by action — one small, intentional shift at a time."
— *LaTarsha Mills-McKie*

🌱 See the Lens

Focus: Identify your default mindset and choose a growth-oriented lens.
Resources:

- 🔖 *Mindset Reflection Sheet* – Recognize fixed vs. growth patterns in real situations.
- 🔍 *See the Lens Journal Prompts* – Reflect on how challenges shape your thinking.
  Inspired by: Dweck (2006), *Mindset: The New Psychology of Success*

- 🎯 **Get Clear on What You Want**

Focus: Define your "why" and set clear, value-driven goals.
Resources:

- *Clarity Map Template* – Align goals with your purpose and core values.
- *Vision Builder Worksheet* – Write a clear vision statement that motivates action.
  Research Insight: Clarity improves commitment and follow-through (Gollwitzer, 1999).

Choose Your Focus Daily

Focus: Direct your attention toward what matters most each day.
Resources:

- *Daily Focus Planner* – Track thoughts, gratitude, and growth opportunities.
- *Shift Reminder Cards* – Quick daily affirmations to reset your mindset.
  Research Insight: Focused attention strengthens neural pathways (Draganski et al., 2004).

Small Wins Create Big Shifts

Focus: Build momentum through consistent micro-actions.
Resources:

- *Small Wins Tracker* – Record progress to boost motivation.
- *Momentum Log* – Celebrate daily progress, not perfection.

Inspired by: Amabile & Kramer (2010), *The Progress Principle.*

💪 Shift Through the Bounce Back

Focus: Reframe failure and practice resilience.
Resources:

- *Bounce Back Blueprint* – Turn setbacks into lessons and action plans.
- *Reframe & Recover Prompts* – Shift from "why me" to "what's next."
  Research Insight: Resilient thinking builds long-term confidence and adaptability.

🔁 Stay in the Shift

Focus: Maintain new habits and identity alignment.
Resources:

- *Habit & Mindset Tracker* – Strengthen consistency and accountability.
- *Stay-in-the-Shift Weekly Review* – Reflect on what's working and adjust with intention.
  Neuroscience Connection: Practice creates new mental pathways — *your brain rewires through repetition.*

💬 Continue the Journey

Resources Beyond the Book:

- 🖥 **Download All Tools:** www.Coachlatarsha.com
- 🎧 **Follow the Shift Happens Podcast** – Coming soon!
- 🤝 **Coaching & Workshops:** www.Coachlatarsha.com
- ✉ **Connect:** LifeCoachL@coachlatarsha.com
- 📱 **Follow:** @CoachL on Instagram & Tik Tok

About the Author-- **LaTarsha Mills-McKie**

LaTarsha Mills-McKie is a Gallup-Certified Strengths Coach, educator, and transformational mindset strategist with over 30 years of experience helping individuals unlock their potential through intentional growth. Known for her heart-centered leadership and practical, research-based approach, she empowers people to shift their thinking, build resilience, and take meaningful action toward their goals.

Throughout her career in education and leadership, LaTarsha has mentored thousands of students, women, and professionals—guiding them to discover their strengths, trust their voice, and show up with confidence. Her coaching blends clarity, compassion, and real-life application, making personal growth both accessible and achievable.

As a speaker and coach, she is dedicated to creating spaces where people can reset, realign, and reclaim the life they want. Her signature philosophy is simple: **small mindset shifts lead to big life results**.

Shift Happens is her invitation to readers to embrace progress over perfection, choose purpose over pressure, and take the small daily steps that transform everything.

LaTarsha lives her mission daily—helping others grow with intention, rise with resilience, and step boldly into the best version of themselves.